Brands We Know

My Little Pony

By Sara Green

Bellwether Media • MI

Jump into the cockpit and take flight with Pilot books. Your journey will take you on high-energy adventures as you learn about all that is wild, weird, fascinating, and fun!

This edition first published in 2018 by Bellwether Media, Inc.

Library of Congress Cataloging-in-Publication Data

Names: Green, Sara, 1964- author.
Title: My Little Pony / by Sara Green.
Description: Minneapolis, MN : Bellwether Media, Inc., [2018] | Series:
  Pilot: Brands We Know | Includes bibliographical references and index.
Identifiers: LCCN 2017031299 (print) | LCCN 2017041181 (ebook) | ISBN
  9781626177758 (hardcover : alk. paper) | ISBN 9781681035147 (ebook)
Subjects: LCSH: My Little Pony (Trademark)--Juvenile literature. | Character
  toys--United States--Juvenile literature. | Toy industry--United
  States--Juvenile literature.
Classification: LCC HD9993.T692 (ebook) | LCC HD9993.T692 G74 2018 (print)|
  DDC 338.4/768872--dc23
LC record available at https://lccn.loc.gov/2017031299

Editor: Betsy Rathburn   Designer: Josh Brink

Printed in the United States of America, North Mankato, MN.

Table of Contents

What Is My Little Pony?.........................4

The Magic Begins.................................6

Fun Across Generations.......................8

Friendship Is Magic.............................14

Fans and Friendship 18

My Little Pony Timeline.......................20

Glossary 22

To Learn More.....................................23

Index...24

What Is My Little Pony?

Twilight Sparkle and Pinkie Pie plan a picnic for their friends. Pinkie Pie bakes cupcakes for dessert. Rainbow Dash decides to play a trick and hides the cupcakes. This makes Pinkie Pie cry. Rainbow Dash feels bad and returns the cupcakes. Everyone is happy! Now the ponies can enjoy a delicious picnic. In the world of My Little Pony, friendship is magic!

My Little Pony is a toy **brand** created by a company called Hasbro. Company **headquarters** is in Pawtucket, Rhode Island. My Little Pony is known for its wide selection of toy ponies. They have colorful bodies and flowing manes. My Little Pony clothes, books, and decorations are popular. The brand's puzzles and playsets are also top sellers. Over time, My Little Pony has expanded to television shows and movies. People around the world love My Little Pony's message of friendship. Today, the brand is worth nearly $200 million!

Generation One pony

By the Numbers

more than
170 countries
broadcast *My Little Pony: Friendship is Magic*

brings in over
$1 billion
in retail sales

1986's *My Little Pony: The Movie* earned
$6 million
at the box office

4
Equestria Girls films

4
generations of My Little Pony

more than
1,000
different ponies

Hasbro Headquarters in Pawtucket, Rhode Island

The Magic Begins

My Little Pony started as a toy called My Pretty Pony. An artist named Bonnie Zacherle created it in 1981 for Hasbro. As a child, Bonnie dreamed of owning a horse. When she grew up, she wanted to share her love of horses with others. This gave her the idea for My Pretty Pony. A **sculptor** named Charles Muenchinger helped design the toy. The brown plastic pony was 10 inches (25.4 centimeters) high. It could wiggle its ears, swish its tail, and wink!

My Pretty Pony

Generation One

Hasbro began making the toy smaller and softer in 1983. They also changed the brand's name to My Little Pony. There were six original ponies. They came in bright colors like pink and purple. People could comb their flowing manes and tails. Special markings were painted on their **flanks**. In time, these would be called cutie marks.

Fun Across Generations

My Little Pony was a huge success. Soon, more ponies were introduced with different features. Pegasus ponies had wings, and Unicorn ponies had horns. Popular Rainbow ponies had colorful stripes on their manes and tails. Children also loved Sparkle ponies. Their bodies were filled with glitter. Different animal types were also introduced. Sea ponies were bath toys that looked like sea horses. Pony Friends were lions, kangaroos, and other animals made in the same style as the ponies.

By the mid-1980s, My Little Pony had its own **animated** television program. The ponies soon made their big-screen **debut** with *My Little Pony: The Movie* in 1986. Despite the brand's success, Hasbro stopped selling My Little Pony in the United States in 1992. Sales continued in other countries until 1995. Hundreds of ponies were introduced between 1982 and 1995. They eventually came to be known as **Generation** One. More than 150 million of these ponies were sold.

Sea pony

My Little Pony

The Movie

Post Office Ponies
Some ponies were only available through the mail. Until 2006, people could collect points to order them for free. Birthflower ponies were popular mail-order ponies. There was one for each month of the year!

Hasbro returned to making My Little Pony in 1997. The new line of ponies came to be known as Generation Two. They were smaller and thinner than Generation One ponies. Their legs and necks were longer. Small, plastic jewels dotted their eyes. This new look was not popular, and the ponies did not sell well. The line was discontinued in the United States in 1998.

You Can Be Anything
2010s-current tagline

Generation Two

Generation Three

Six years later, Hasbro changed the ponies again. Their bodies became rounder and their legs shorter. Hearts, stars, and other shapes were painted on each pony's eyes. Most ponies had shiny bodies with cutie marks on one side. These ponies were known as Generation Three. Hasbro made many special ponies during this generation. Dress-up Eveningwear ponies came with fancy outfits. Newborn Cutie ponies wore diapers! Generation Three was very successful. Around 100 million ponies were sold by 2010.

Custom Ponies

A custom pony is a pony that someone has changed for artistic reasons. Sometimes people paint new cutie marks or change the body color. They may add colors to the manes and tails. They can even sculpt wings or unicorn horns!

Hasbro launched Generation Four in 2010. It started with an animated television series called *My Little Pony: Friendship is Magic*. This hit series features six ponies. Pinkie Pie and Applejack are Earth ponies. Rainbow Dash and Fluttershy are Pegasus ponies. Rarity is a Unicorn. Twilight Sparkle begins as a Unicorn but later becomes an Alicorn. She has wings and a horn! Together, all six ponies are known as the Mane 6.

The series takes place in Ponyville, a town in the land of Equestria. There, the ponies have adventures and learn about friendship. They use the Elements of Harmony to keep Ponyville safe from danger. These special **artifacts** represent six important parts of friendship. For example, Applejack's artifact is a gold necklace with an apple-shaped orange gem. It stands for honesty. Her friends count on her to always tell the truth. Pinkie Pie's necklace has a blue gem. It represents laughter! She brings fun wherever she goes. When used together, the Elements of Harmony are very powerful!

Guest Stars

Many famous people have guest starred on *My Little Pony: Friendship is Magic*. Musician Weird Al Yankovic provided the voice for a pony named Cheese Sandwich!

Weird Al Yankovic

The Mane 6

Character	Type of Pony	Element of Harmony
Applejack	Earth	Honesty
Fluttershy	Pegasus	Kindness
Pinkie Pie	Earth	Laughter
Rainbow Dash	Pegasus	Loyalty
Rarity	Unicorn	Generosity
Twilight Sparkle	Alicorn	Magic

Fluttershy

Rainbow Dash

Applejack

Twilight Sparkle

Rarity

Pinkie Pie

Friendship Is Magic

My Little Pony: Friendship is Magic features many other characters besides the Mane 6. Spike is a baby dragon who can breathe green fire. He is Twilight Sparkle's best friend and assistant. Princess Celestia is the ruler of Equestria. She is an Alicorn who raises the sun and the moon. The Cutie Mark Crusaders are young ponies. Their story begins before they have cutie marks. As time goes on, they learn that helping others is what matters most. This discovery helps them earn their marks!

Pony Puns

The characters in *My Little Pony: Friendship is Magic* have their own vocabulary. For example, they say "anypony" instead of anybody and "somepony" instead of somebody.

Friendship is Magic

current tagline

Princess Luna

Princess Celestia

Some characters are not always kind. Princess Celestia's sister, Princess Luna, was once known as Nightmare Moon. She stopped the sun from shining on Equestria. A character named Discord behaved in selfish, reckless ways. He enjoyed causing trouble. Queen Chrysalis could change her shape to confuse others. She wanted total control of Equestria. Over time, many of these characters made positive changes. Others still have lessons to learn!

Discord

My Little Pony characters star in movies, too. In 2017, *My Little Pony: The Movie* hit theaters. It stars the *Friendship is Magic* ponies. There have been other movies, too. In 2013, Hasbro introduced the Equestria Girls in a movie called *My Little Pony: Equestria Girls*. The Equestria Girls are teens with personalities based on the *Friendship is Magic* characters. The girls look like humans in most ways except for their **pastel** skin colors. In the movie, Twilight Sparkle chases an enemy into a new world and finds herself in a high school. There, she is shocked to find she and her pony friends have changed into humans. Magic and adventure soon fill their lives!

Other movies feature the Equestria Girls, too. The characters face off in exciting competitions in *Rainbow Rocks* and *Friendship Games*. In *Legend of Everfree*, the girls discover a magical force. The Equestria Girls line includes toys, movies, and television programs. It also has its own music and an **app**.

Equestria Girl

Fans and Friendship

My Little Pony: Friendship is Magic was originally aimed at young girls. However, many other people have grown to love the series. They enjoy its characters, messages, and humor. Fans celebrate the series in many ways. They create web sites and videos. Many attend My Little Pony **conventions**. Fans enjoy meeting each other and discussing the show. Some even wear My Little Pony costumes!

My Little Pony convention

My Little Pony inspires friendship in other ways, too. The brand celebrated International Day of Friendship in 2016 with a special **campaign**. It encouraged people to do kind things for others. In this way, people would "friend it forward." Fans could share their acts of kindness on **social networks**. Hasbro also donated money to an organization called Points of Light. It inspires people around the world to **volunteer** in their communities. My Little Pony brings friendship and happiness to people all over the world!

A Happy Surprise
McDonald's offered My Little Pony toys in some Happy Meals in 2017. The ponies included Rainbow Dash, Twilight Sparkle, and Pinkie Pie.

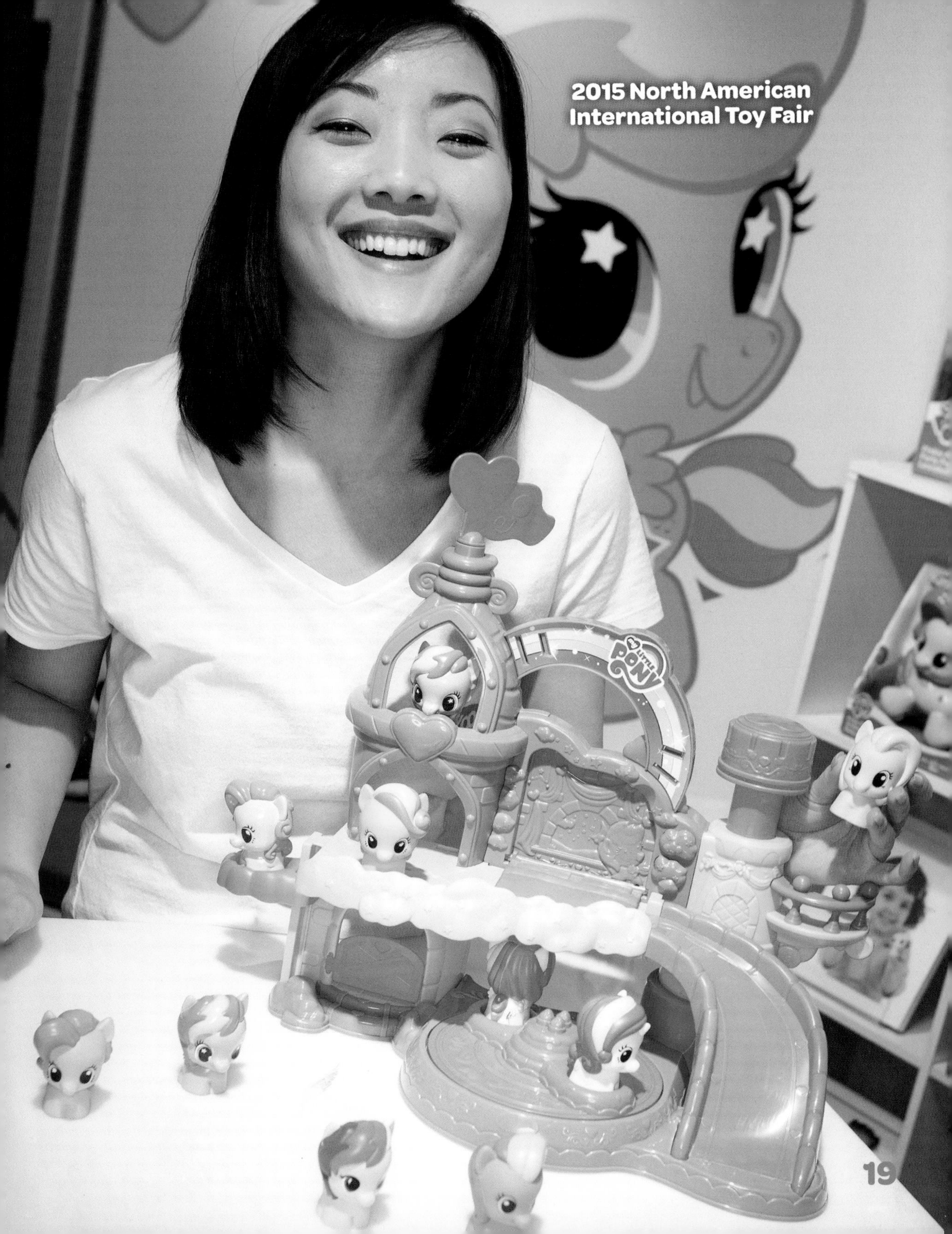

2015 North American International Toy Fair

My Little Pony Timeline

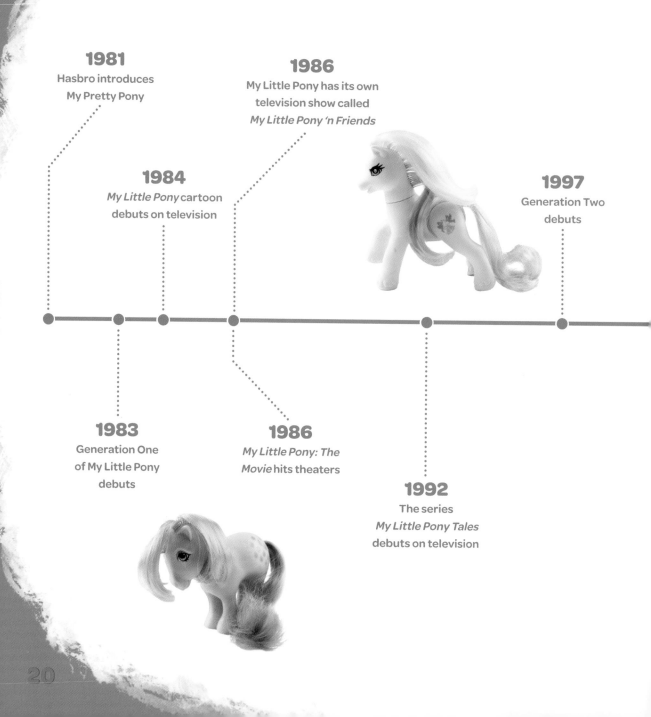

1981
Hasbro introduces
My Pretty Pony

1986
My Little Pony has its own
television show called
My Little Pony 'n Friends

1984
My Little Pony cartoon
debuts on television

1997
Generation Two
debuts

1983
Generation One
of My Little Pony
debuts

1986
*My Little Pony: The
Movie* hits theaters

1992
The series
My Little Pony Tales
debuts on television

2003

Generation Three debuts

2013

Equestria Girls are introduced
in a film called *My Little Pony:
Equestria Girls*

2010

*My Little Pony:
Friendship is Magic*
debuts

2015

*Equestria Girls:
Friendship Games*
is released

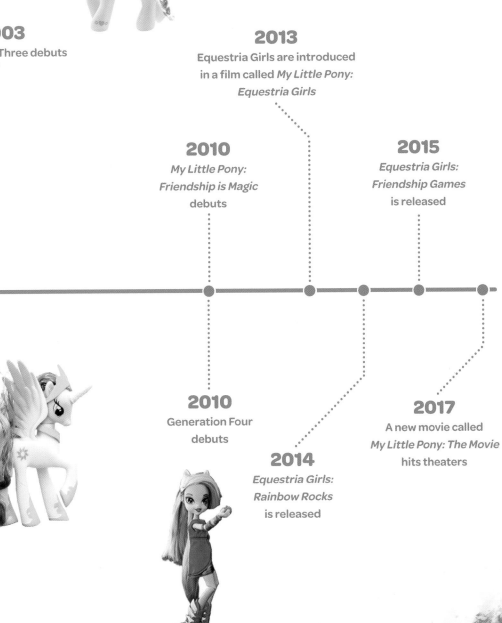

2010

Generation Four
debuts

2017

A new movie called
My Little Pony: The Movie
hits theaters

2014

*Equestria Girls:
Rainbow Rocks*
is released

Glossary

animated—produced by the creation of a series of drawings that are shown quickly, one after the other, to give the appearance of movement

apps—a small, specialized program downloaded onto smartphones and other mobile devices

artifacts—objects and ornaments made to represent different things

brand—a category of products all made by the same company

campaign—a series of activities that are meant to achieve a particular goal

conventions—large meetings where people gather to discuss and learn about common interests

debut—a first-time introduction

flanks—areas on the side of an animal's body between the ribs and hip

generation—a class of objects developed at about the same time

headquarters—a company's main office

pastel—a soft, delicate shade of a color

sculptor—an artist who makes three-dimensional art using clay, wood, metal, and other substances

social networks—web sites or apps that help users communicate by sharing messages and pictures

volunteer—to do something for others without expecting money or goods in return

To Learn More

AT THE LIBRARY

DK Publishing. *The Amazing Book of My Little Pony*. DK Publishing, 2017.

Green, Sara. *Parker Brothers*. Minneapolis, Minn.: Bellwether Media, 2017.

Snider, Brandon T. *The Elements of Harmony: Friendship is Magic*. Little, Brown and Company, 2013.

ON THE WEB

Learning more about My Little Pony is as easy as 1, 2, 3.

1. Go to www.factsurfer.com.

2. Enter "My Little Pony" into the search box.

3. Click the "Surf" button and you will see a list of related web sites.

With factsurfer.com, finding more information is just a click away.

Index

app, 17

brand, 4, 7, 8, 18

by the numbers, 5

characters, 4, 12, 13, 14, 15, 16, 17, 18

conventions, 18

cutie marks, 7, 11, 14

Equestria Girls, 5, 16, 17

generations, 4, 5, 7, 8, 10, 11, 12

Hasbro, 4, 5, 6, 7, 8, 10, 11, 12, 16, 18

history, 5, 6, 7, 8, 9, 10, 11, 12, 16, 18

International Day of Friendship, 18

Mane 6, 12, 13

movies, 4, 5, 8, 16, 17

Muenchinger, Charles, 6

My Little Pony: Friendship is Magic, 5, 12, 14, 15, 16, 18

My Pretty Pony, 6

Pawtucket, Rhode Island, 4, 5

ponies, 4, 5, 6, 7, 8, 9, 10, 11, 12, 13, 14, 16, 18

products, 4, 6, 7, 8, 9, 10, 11, 17, 18

sales, 5, 8, 10, 11

taglines, 9, 10, 17

television shows, 4, 5, 8, 12, 14, 17, 18

timeline, 20-21

United States, 8, 10

worth, 4

Yankovic, Weird Al, 12

Zacherle, Bonnie, 6